Happy Mother's Day!

Love,
Matthew
and Kat

W9-BQT-229

Psalm 113:9 ~ "He settles the
woman in her home as
a happy mother of children."

2003

CELEBRATING

Mothers

CELEBRATING
Mothers

A Book of Appreciation

EDITED BY

Glorya Hale
and Carol Kelly-Gangi

MetroBooks

2002 MetroBooks

ISBN I-58663-582-4

Book design by Rhea Braunstein

Illustrations by Paul Hoffman

Printed and bound in the United States of America

02 03 04 05 06 MC 9 8 7 6 5 4 3 2

KP

Contents

Introduction

Throughout history, many of the world's outstanding writers and statesmen, artists and actors, inventors and scientists have extolled the attributes of their own mothers and proudly acknowledged their lifelong influence. And women from all over the world and from all walks of life have described the joys and the difficulties of being mothers.

Celebrating Mothers is a collection of memorable quotations about mothers and motherhood. Abraham Lincoln, Henry Kissinger, Maya Angelou, and Mark Twain are among those who pay tribute to their mothers. Anne Morrow Lindbergh, Liv Ullmann, and Margaret Drabble remember the wonder and happiness of when their children were born. Such outstanding women as Barbara Kingsolver, Sophia Loren, and Jacqueline Kennedy Onassis write about the responsibilities of having children. And men and women, including Alice Walker, Russell Baker, Bill Cosby, and Eudora Welty, recount loving anecdotes about their mothers.

This book is truly a celebration of mothers and motherhood. It is hoped that it will be enjoyed and treasured by every mother who reads it.

GLORYA HALE
Albuquerque, New Mexico, 2001

Thanks, Mom

A mother is not a person to lean on but a person to make leaning unnecessary.

DOROTHY CANFIELD FISHER, *American novelist*

Most of all the other beautiful things in life come by twos and threes, by dozens and hundreds. Plenty of roses, stars, sunsets, rainbows, brothers and sisters, aunts and cousins, comrades and friends—but only one mother in the whole world.

KATE DOUGLAS WIGGIN, *American writer*

Youth fades; love droops; the leaves of friendship fall;
A mother's secret hope outlives them all.

OLIVER WENDELL HOLMES, *American man of letters*

Women as the guardians of children possess great power. They are the molders of their children's personalities and the arbiters of their development.

ANN OAKLEY, English sociologist

The future destiny of the child is always the work of the mother.

NAPOLEON BONAPARTE, emperor of France

Most mothers are instinctive philosophers.

HARRIET BEECHER STOWE, American writer

God gives us friends, and that means much;
    But far above all others,
The greatest of his gifts to earth
    Was when He thought of Mothers.

Author Unknown

A mother's love for her child is like nothing else in the world. It knows no law, no pity, it dares all things and crushes down remorselessly all that stands in its path.

From "The Last Séance" by AGATHA CHRISTIE

There is in all this cold and hollow world
No fount of deep, strong, deathless love;
Save that within a mother's heart.

FELICIA HEMANS, *English poet*

I think it must somewhere be written that the virtues of mothers shall be visited on their children.

CHARLES DICKENS, *English novelist*

Romance fails us—and so do friendships—but the relationship of mother and child remains indelible and indestructible—the strongest bond upon this earth.

Theodor Reik, Austrian-born American psychoanalyst

When we see great men and women we give credit to their mothers.

Charlotte Perkins Gilman, American social critic and poet

The bearing and training of a child is woman's wisdom.

Alfred, Lord Tennyson, English poet

Mothers . . . are basically a patient lot. They have to be or they would devour their offspring early on, like guppies.

Mary Daheim, American writer

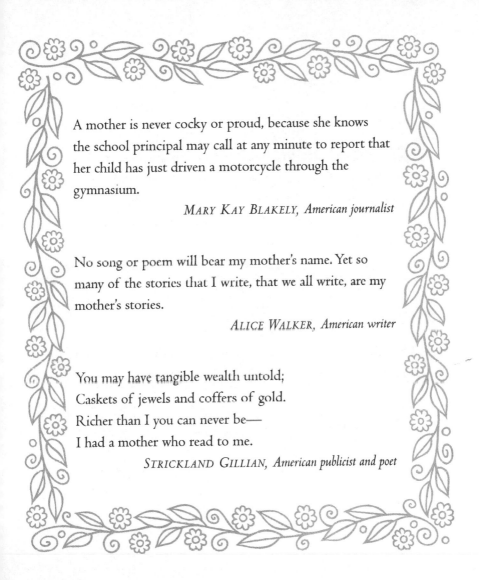

A mother is never cocky or proud, because she knows the school principal may call at any minute to report that her child has just driven a motorcycle through the gymnasium.

MARY KAY BLAKELY, American journalist

No song or poem will bear my mother's name. Yet so many of the stories that I write, that we all write, are my mother's stories.

ALICE WALKER, American writer

You may have tangible wealth untold;
Caskets of jewels and coffers of gold.
Richer than I you can never be—
I had a mother who read to me.

STRICKLAND GILLIAN, American publicist and poet

A mother understands what a child does not say.

Jewish Proverb

The child, in the decisive first years of his life, has the experience of his mother, as an all-enveloping, protective, nourishing power. Mother is food; she is love; she is warmth; she is earth. To be loved by her means to be alive, to be rooted, to be at home.

ERICH FROMM, *German-born American psychiatrist*

Mother is the name for God in the lips and hearts of children.

WILLIAM M. THACKERAY, *English novelist*

A mother is a mother still,
The holiest thing alive.

SAMUEL T. COLERIDGE, *English poet and critic*

God could not be everywhere, so He made mothers.

Jewish Proverb

Her children arise up and call her blessed.

Proverbs 31:28

She brings the sunshine into the house; it is now a pleasure to be there.

CECIL BEATON, *English photographer and designer*

She was ignorant of life and the world, but possessed a heart full of love.

HANS CHRISTIAN ANDERSEN, *Danish writer*

If evolution really works, how come mothers only have two hands?

MILTON BERLE, *American comedian*

By and large, mothers and housewives are the only workers who do not have regular time off. They are the great vacationless class.

  ANNE MORROW LINDBERGH, American writer and aviator

There is no supporter like your mother. Right or wrong, from her viewpoint you are always right.

  HARRY S. TRUMAN, 33rd president of the United States

Holy as heaven a mother's tender love, the love of many prayers and many tears which changes not with dim, declining years.

  CAROLINE NORTON, English writer and poet

Just as breast milk cannot be duplicated, neither can a mother.

  SALLY E. SHAYWITZ, American pediatrician and writer

The mother's heart is the child's schoolroom.

HENRY WARD BEECHER, American clergyman

When you educate a man you educate an individual; when you educate a woman you educate a whole family.

CHARLES D. MCIVER, American university president

Of all the rights of woman, the greatest is to be a mother.

LIN YUTANG, Chinese writer

For the hand that rocks the cradle
Is the hand that rules the world.

WILLIAM ROSS WALLACE, American poet

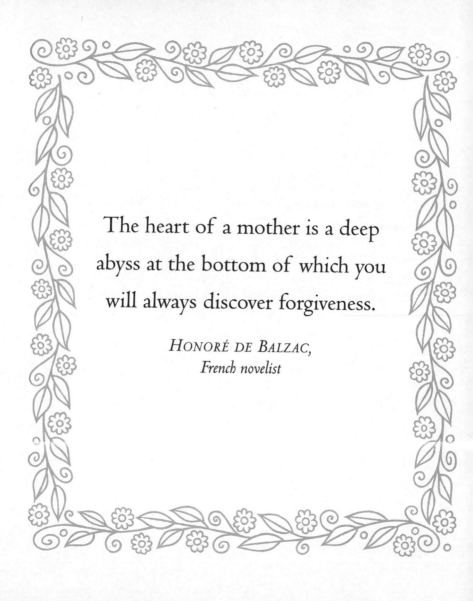

The heart of a mother is a deep abyss at the bottom of which you will always discover forgiveness.

HONORÉ DE BALZAC,
French novelist

A Mother Is . . .

Biology is the least of what makes someone a mother.

OPRAH WINFREY, *American talk-show host and actor*

There is nothing more thrilling in the world, I think, than having a child that is yours, and yet is mysteriously a stranger.

AGATHA CHRISTIE, *English writer*

My evolution into a politician developed not in opposition to my role as a mother, but as an extension of it.

MADELEINE KUNIN, *American politician*

Motherhood means giving.

CHARLOTTE PERKINS GILMAN, *American social critic and poet*

Motherhood is like Albania—you can't trust the descriptions in the books, you have to go there.

MARNI JACKSON, Canadian writer and journalist

Motherhood is neither a duty nor a privilege, but simply the way that humanity can satisfy the desire for physical immortality and triumph over the fear of death.

REBECCA WEST, English writer

Sometimes the strength of motherhood is greater than natural laws.

BARBARA KINGSOLVER, American novelist

Motherhood has a very humanizing effect. Everything gets reduced to essentials.

MERYL STREEP, American actor

No matter how old a mother is she watches her middle-aged children for signs of improvement.

FLORIDA SCOTT-MAXWELL, American psychologist and actor

I was once present when an old mother, who had brought up a large family of children with eminent success, was asked by a young one what she would recommend in the case of some children who were too anxiously educated, and her reply was—"I think, my dear, a little wholesome neglect."

SIR HENRY TAYLOR, English poet

When her biographer says of an Italian woman poet, "during some years her Muse was intermitted," we do not wonder at the fact when he casually mentions her ten children.

ANNA GARLIN SPENCER, American minister and journalist

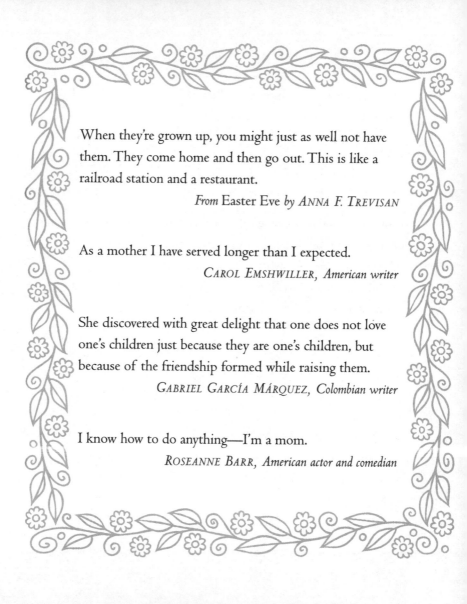

When they're grown up, you might just as well not have them. They come home and then go out. This is like a railroad station and a restaurant.

From Easter Eve *by* ANNA F. TREVISAN

As a mother I have served longer than I expected.

CAROL EMSHWILLER, *American writer*

She discovered with great delight that one does not love one's children just because they are one's children, but because of the friendship formed while raising them.

GABRIEL GARCÍA MÁRQUEZ, *Colombian writer*

I know how to do anything—I'm a mom.

ROSEANNE BARR, *American actor and comedian*

It's frightening to think that you mark your children merely by being yourself. It seems unfair. You can't assume the responsibility for everything you do—or don't do.

SIMONE DE BEAUVOIR, French writer and philosopher

My children cause me the most exquisite suffering of which I have any experience. It is the suffering of ambivalence: the murderous alternation between bitter resentment and raw-edged nerves, and blissful gratification and tenderness.

ADRIENNE RICH, American poet and educator

It's always been my feeling that God lends you your children until they're about eighteen years old. If you haven't made your points with them by then, it's too late.

BETTY FORD, American first lady

Though motherhood is the most important of all the professions—requiring more knowledge than any other department in human affairs—there was no attention given to preparation of this office.

ELIZABETH CADY STANTON, American suffragist and historian

You can never really live anyone else's life, not even your child's. The influence you exert is through your own life, and what you've become yourself.

ELEANOR ROOSEVELT, American first lady and writer

[A mother] never quite leaves her children at home, even when she doesn't take them along.

MARGARET CULKIN BANNING, American writer

Before becoming a mother I had a hundred theories on how to bring up children. Now I have seven children and only one theory: love them, especially when they least deserve to be loved.

KATE SAMPERI, author

Loving a child is a circular business. The more you give the more you get, the more you want to give.

PENELOPE LEACH, American pediatrician

Children are likely to live up to what you believe of them.

LADY BIRD JOHNSON, American first lady

Learning how to be a mother is not a matter of adopting a certain set of attitudes, but of expressing one's own personality in the task of responding flexibly to the child's needs.

SHEILA KITZINGER, English writer

When you are a mother, you are never really alone in your thoughts. You are connected to your child and to all those who touch your lives. A mother always has to think twice, once for herself and once for her child.

SOPHIA LOREN, Italian actor

More than in any other human relationship, overwhelmingly more, motherhood means being instantly interruptible, responsive, responsible.

TILLIE OLSEN, American writer

Motherhood affords an instant identity. First, through wifehood, you are somebody's wife; then you are somebody's mother. Both give not only identity and activity, but status and stardom of a kind.

BETSY ROLLIN, American writer, editor, and actor

Because I am a mother, I am capable of being shocked; as I never was when I was not one.

MARGARET ATWOOD, Canadian writer

If you bungle raising your children, I don't think whatever else you do well matters very much.

JACQUELINE KENNEDY ONASSIS, American first lady and editor

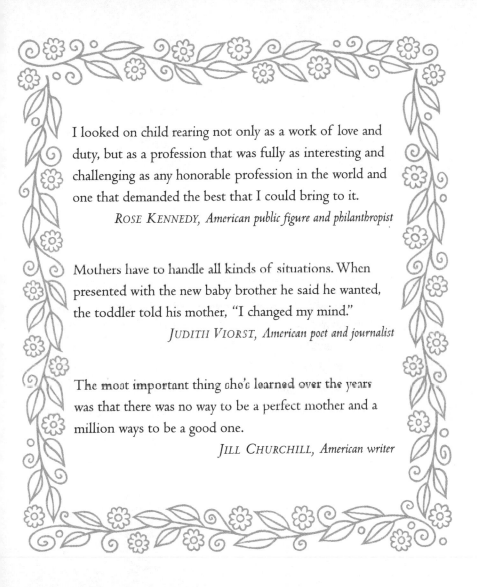

I looked on child rearing not only as a work of love and duty, but as a profession that was fully as interesting and challenging as any honorable profession in the world and one that demanded the best that I could bring to it.

ROSE KENNEDY, *American public figure and philanthropist*

Mothers have to handle all kinds of situations. When presented with the new baby brother he said he wanted, the toddler told his mother, "I changed my mind."

JUDITH VIORST, *American poet and journalist*

The most important thing she's learned over the years was that there was no way to be a perfect mother and a million ways to be a good one.

JILL CHURCHILL, *American writer*

Nothing else ever will make you as happy or as sad, as proud or as tired, for nothing is quite as hard as helping a person develop his own individuality—especially while you struggle to keep your own.

From The Mother's Almanac
by MARGUERITE KELLY and ELIA PARSONS

Trivial things and important things wound into and against one another, all warring for her attention. Changing the goldfish water wasn't vital, but it couldn't wait; teaching the children their Bible was vital, but it could wait. Listening to them, growing with them, that was vital; but the bills had to be paid now, the dinner was burning right now.

From "Children of Joy" by JOANNE GREENBERG

I figure when my husband comes home from work, if the kids are still alive, then I've done my job.

ROSEANNE BARR, American comedian and actor

Pregnancy doubled her, birth halved her, and motherhood turned her into Everywoman.

From Parachutes & Kisses *by* ERICA JONG

There never was a child so lovely but his mother was glad to get him asleep.

RALPH WALDO EMERSON, *American essayist and philosopher*

No one but doctors and mothers know what it means to have interruptions.

KARL A. MENNINGER, *American psychiatrist*

There are two kinds of mothers: those who place a child's bouquet in a milk bottle on top of the refrigerator, and those who enthrone it in a vase on the piano.

MARCELENE COX, *American writer*

Some are kissing mothers and some are scolding mothers, but it is love just the same, and most mothers kiss and scold together.

PEARL S. BUCK, American novelist

I'm going to stop punishing my children by saying, "Never mind! I'll do it myself."

ERMA BOMBECK, American humorist

Likely as not, the child you can do least with will do the most to make you proud.

MIGNON MCLAUGHLIN, American journalist

The way to rear up children (to be just),
They know a simple, merry, tender knack
Of tying sashes, fitting baby shoes,
And stringing pretty words that make no sense,
And kissing full sense into empty words.

ELIZABETH BARRETT BROWNING, English poet

Often as a parent raising children, especially a son, I have wished for a guidebook, a map to direct me through the labyrinth of the human emotional field, to cleanly and gracefully assist my children through the hills and valleys of achievements and failures. I have learned that the only guidebook of any effectiveness is the human heart.

JOY HARJO, Creek writer and poet

There are lots of things that you can brush under the carpet about yourself until you're faced with somebody whose needs won't be put off.

ANGELA CARTER, English writer

Maternity is on the face of it an unsocial experience. The selfishness that a woman has learned to stifle or to dissemble when she is alone blooms freely and unashamed on behalf of her offspring.

EMILY JAMES PUTNAM, American educator and writer

Our children are not going to be just "our children"—they are going to be other people's husbands and wives and the parents of our grandchildren.

Mary S. Calderone,
American physician and public health educator

What do you do with mother love and wit when the babies are grown and gone away?

Joanne Greenberg, American writer

These remarkable women of olden times are like the ancient painted glass—the art of making them is lost; my mother was less than her mother, and I am less than my mother.

Harriet Beecher Stowe, American writer

My children . . . have been a constant joy to me (except on the days when they weren't).

Evelyn Fairbanks, American writer and educator

It's good to sit in one's house with a child playing outside quite safely, quite happily. There aren't many better sensations in life.

EMILY HAHN, American writer

The mother's battle for her child—with sickness, with poverty, with war, with all the forces of exploitation and callousness that cheapen human life—needs to become a common human battle, waged in love and in the passion for survival.

ADRIENNE RICH, American poet and educator

Sometimes when I look at all my children, I say to myself, "Lillian, you should have stayed a virgin."

LILLIAN CARTER, mother of President Jimmy Carter

Working Moms

Being asked to decide between your passion for work and your passion for children was like being asked by your doctor whether you preferred him to remove your brain or your heart.

MARY KAY BLAKELY, American writer and journalist

So many women have chosen lives of seeming contradictions. I remember mentioning the baby sitter in a column once and receiving outraged letters from readers who could not understand how anyone who could write feelingly of her children would hire help with their care. When did those people think I was writing? In the checkout line at the supermarket?

ANNA QUINDLEN, American columnist and novelist

At work you think of the children you've left at home. At home you think of the work you've left unfinished. Such a struggle is unleashed within yourself: your heart is rent.

GOLDA MEIR, *Russian-born Israeli prime minister and politician*

Reminds me of what one of mine wrote in a third-grade piece on how her mother spent her time. She reported "one half time on home, one half time on outside things, one half time writing."

CHARLOTTE MONTGOMERY, *American writer and columnist*

When I had my daughter, I learned what the sound of one hand clapping is—it's a woman holding an infant in one arm and a pen in the other.

KATE BRAVERMAN, *American poet, writer, and performance artist*

[Children] use up the same part of my head as poetry does. To deal with children is a matter of terrific imaginative identification. And the children have to come first. It's no use putting off their evening meal for two months.

LIBBY HOUSTON, English poet and broadcaster

I'm real ambivalent about [working mothers]. Those of us who have been in the women's movement for a long time know that we've talked a good game of "go out and fulfill your dreams" and "be everything you were meant to be." But by the same token, we want daughters-in-law who are going to stay home and raise our grandchildren.

ERMA BOMBECK, American humorist

She was a beautiful baby. She blew shining bubbles of sound.
She loved motion, loved light, loved color and music and
textures. . . . She was a miracle to me, but when she was
eight months old I had to leave her daytimes with the
woman downstairs to whom she was no miracle at all.

TILLIE OLSEN, American writer

It seems to me that since I've had children, I've grown richer
and deeper. They may have slowed down my writing for a
while, but when I did write, I had more of a self to speak
from.

ANNE TYLER, American novelist

My mother taught me. She taught me about family and hard
work and sacrifice. She held steady through tragedy after
tragedy. . . . I watched her go off to work each day at a time
when it wasn't always easy to be a working mother.

BILL CLINTON, 42nd president of the United States

The Blessed Event

Making the decision to have a child—it's momentous. It is to decide forever to have your heart go walking outside your body.

ELIZABETH STONE, *American writer*

I will never forget my blissful joy when I was first sure that I was pregnant.

DOROTHY DAY, *American social activist and pacifist*

I never feel so good as when I'm pregnant. It's the only time a woman can sit still, do nothing at all, and be beautifully productive.

MARIA RIVA, *American actor*

The street's abloom with pregnant women. They stand next to me in elevators. I see them on movie lines, getting out of taxicabs, choosing fruit and vegetables. . . . Were they here before I was pregnant? Will they all disappear when I give birth? After that, will I only notice new mothers and new babies?

PHYLLIS CHESLER, American psychiatrist

The biggest problem facing a pregnant woman is not nausea or fatigue or her wardrobe—it's free advice.

SOPHIA LOREN, Italian actor

If I could only *feel* the child! I imagine the moment of its quickening as a sudden awakening of my own being which has never before had life. I want to *live* with the child, and I am as heavy as a stone.

EVELYN SCOTT, American writer

When I was pregnant with Josephine I told Mother, "All I could possibly hope for with my children is that they love me as much as I love you."

MADELEINE L'ENGLE, American writer and teacher

Men never think, at least seldom think, what a hard task it is for us women to go through this very often. God's will be done, and if He decrees that we are to have a great many children why we must try to bring them up as useful and exemplary members of society.

QUEEN VICTORIA, Queen of England

While marriage is a parting, an exile from the maternal home, giving birth is a time to return, to celebrate, to feast on rich nutty sweets, to imbibe life-giving proteins, to have your body, numb after childbirth, rubbed over with hot oils and unguents steeped in herbs.

MEENA ALEXANDER, Indian-born American writer

Before you were conceived I wanted you
Before you were born I loved you
Before you were here an hour I would die for you
This is the miracle of life.

> MAUREEN HAWKINS, *poet*

My darling little girl-child, after such a long and
troublesome waiting I now have you in my arms. I am alone
no more. I have my baby.

> MARTHA MARTIN, *American diarist and adventurer*

For any normal woman in normal circumstances there is
bound to be a special excitement and joy and gratitude to
God when she holds her first baby in her arms.

> ROSE KENNEDY, *American public figure and philanthropist*

When they brought the baby in to her . . . she stared, inert,
and thought, This is the author of my pain.

> *From* The Actress *by* BESSIE BREUER

I looked at this tiny, perfect creature and it was as though a light switch had been turned on. A great rush of love flooded out of me.

MADELEINE L'ENGLE, *American writer and teacher*

I stood in the hospital the night after she was born. Through a window I could see all the small, crying newborn infants and somewhere among them slept the one who was mine. I stood there for hours filled with happiness until the night nurse sent me to bed.

LIV ULLMANN, *Norwegian actress*

As often as I have witnessed the miracle, held the perfect creature with its tiny hands and feet, each time I have felt as though I were entering a cathedral with prayer in my heart.

MARGARET SANGER, *American nurse and birth control reformer*

In the sheltered simplicity of the first days after a baby is born, one sees again the magical closed circle, the miraculous sense of two people existing only for each other, the tranquil sky reflected on the face of the mother nursing her child.

ANNE MORROW LINDBERGH, *American writer and aviator*

I think my life began with waking up and loving my mother's face.

From Daniel Deronda *by* GEORGE ELIOT

Upon her soothing breast
She lulled her little child;
A winter sunset in the west,
A dreary glory smiled.

EMILY BRONTË, *English writer*

Maternity is common, but not so
It seemed to me. Motherless, I did not know—
I was all unprepared to feel this glow. . . .

ALICE DUER MILLER, *American poet*

Who is getting more pleasure from this rocking, the baby or me?

NANCY THAYER, American writer

When you have a baby, you set off an explosion in your marriage, and when the dust settles, your marriage is different from what it was. Not better, necessarily; not worse, necessarily; but different.

NORA EPHRON, American writer

What is the road to slumber land and when does the
   baby go?
The road lies straight through mother's arms when the sun
   is sinking low.

MARY DOW BRINE, American poet

There is amazed curiosity in every young mother. It is strangely miraculous to see and hold a living being formed within oneself.

SIMONE DE BEAUVOIR, French writer and philosopher

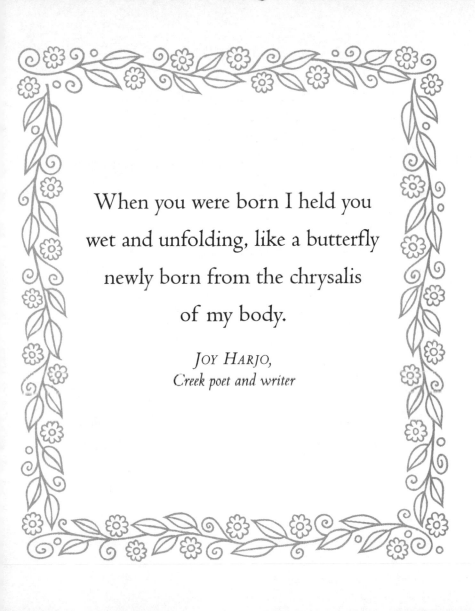

When you were born I held you
wet and unfolding, like a butterfly
newly born from the chrysalis
of my body.

JOY HARJO,
Creek poet and writer

I actually remember feeling delight, at two o'clock in the morning, when the baby woke for his feed, because I so longed to have another look at him.

MARGARET DRABBLE, *English novelist*

I love this little life! With all the pain of it, I long for a tiny human creature to spring from between my limbs bravely out into the world. I need it, just as a true poet *needs* to create a great undying work.

YANG PING, *Chinese writer*

He was too young to want milk but I held his face against my breast. In all my desire for him I was conscious of a heavy sensuality, a massiveness of appreciation.

EVELYN SCOTT, *American writer*

I felt [then] as I do now, that every mother ought to learn to care for her own baby, whether she can afford to delegate the task to someone else or not.

SARA ROOSEVELT, mother of President Franklin Delano Roosevelt

I dream of birthdays to come. Of celebrating your birth anew. Celebrating when you became separate, distinct from me, my body—became part of this world.

JEWELL PARKER RHODES, American writer

Soft sleepy mouth so vaguely pressed
Against your new-made mother's breast.
Soft little hands in mine I fold,
Soft little feet I kiss and hold,
Round soft smooth head and tiny ear,
All mine, my own, my baby dear.

EDITH NESBITT, English writer and poet

I nursed my son, marveling how I could have lived thirty-five years on this earth without reading a description of the throat-clotting tenderness a nursing mother can feel. I came to think that nothing in life was more important than a parent's love for her child. . . .

EILEEN POLLACK, American writer and educator

There is no other closeness in human life like the closeness between a mother and her baby—chronologically, physically, and spiritually they are just a few heartbeats away from being the same person.

SUSAN CHEEVER, American writer

Whenever I held my newborn babe in my arms, I used to think what I did and what I said to him would have an influence, not only on him, but on everyone he meets, not for a day, or a year, but for all time and for eternity. What a challenge, what a joy!

ROSE KENNEDY, American public figure and philanthropist

Mothers and Daughters

I am a reflection of my mother's secret poetry as well as of her hidden angers.

AUDRE LORDE, *West Indian-born American poet, writer, and critic*

I wonder why you care so much about me — no, I don't wonder. I only accept it as the thing at the back of all one's life that makes everything bearable and possible.

GERTRUDE BELL, *English traveler and political figure*

Thou art thy mother's glass, and she in thee
Calls back the lovely April of her prime.

WILLIAM SHAKESPEARE, *English dramatist*

Yes, Mother . . . I can see you are flawed. You have not
hidden it. That is your greatest gift to me.

ALICE WALKER, American writer

Whenever I'm with my mother, I feel as though I have to
spend the whole time avoiding land mines.

From The Kitchen God's Wife *by AMY TAN*

My mother was my first jealous lover.

BARBARA GRIZZUTI HARRISON, American writer and publicist

My mother and I could always look out the same window
without ever seeing the same thing.

GLORIA SWANSON, American actor

Mother of my granddaughter,
Listen to my song:
A mother can't do right,
A daughter can't be wrong.

URSULA K. LE GUIN, American writer and literary critic

Don't ever forget all mothers were once daughters.

JANE O'REILLY, American writer

As is the mother, so is her daughter.

The Bible

Daughter am I in my mother's house;
But mistress in my own.

RUDYARD KIPLING, English writer and poet

My mother is a woman who speaks with her life as much as
with her tongue.

KESAYA E. NODA, American writer

To describe my mother would be to write about a hurricane in its perfect power.

MAYA ANGELOU, American writer and poet

Guided by my heritage of a love of beauty and a respect for strength—in search of my mother's garden, I found my own.

ALICE WALKER, American writer

Blushing, full of confusion, I talked with her
   about my
worries and the fear in my body. I fell on her
   breast,
and all over again I became a little girl sobbing
   in her
arms at the terror of life.

GABRIELA MISTRAL, Chilean poet

I know her face by heart. Sometimes I think nothing will break her spell.

DAPHNE MERKIN, American writer

I fear, as any daughter would, losing myself back into the mother.

KIM CHERNIN, American writer

I have reached the age when a woman begins to perceive that she is growing into the person she least plans to resemble: her mother.

ANITA BROOKNER, English writer

My mother wanted me to be her wings, to fly as she never quite had the courage to do.

ERICA JONG, American writer and poet

Living with her was like being on a journey of discovery that never ended.

ELIZABETH GOUDGE, English novelist

I want to lean into her the way wheat leans into wind.

From The Beet Queen *by LOUISE ERDRICH*

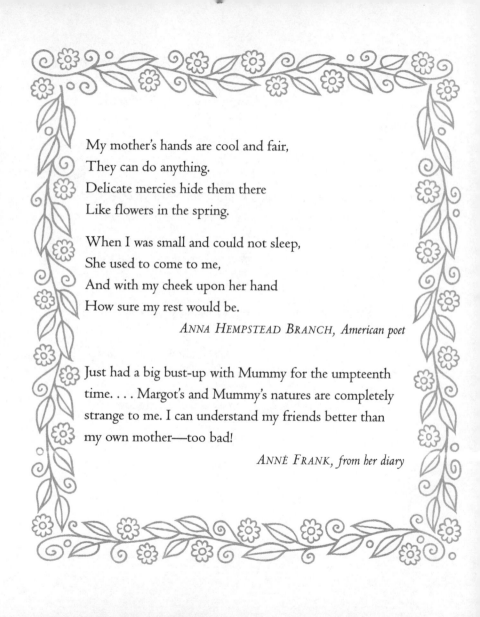

My mother's hands are cool and fair,
They can do anything.
Delicate mercies hide them there
Like flowers in the spring.

When I was small and could not sleep,
She used to come to me,
And with my cheek upon her hand
How sure my rest would be.

ANNA HEMPSTEAD BRANCH, American poet

Just had a big bust-up with Mummy for the umpteenth
time. . . . Margot's and Mummy's natures are completely
strange to me. I can understand my friends better than
my own mother—too bad!

ANNE FRANK, from her diary

And it came to me, and I knew what I had to have before
my soul would rest. I want to belong—to belong to my
mother. And in return—I wanted my mother to belong
to me.

Gloria Vanderbilt, American artist and designer

Out of the corner of one eye, I could see my mother. Out
of the corner of the other eye, I could see her shadow on
the wall, cast there by the lamplight. It was a big and solid
shadow, and it looked so much like my mother that I
became frightened. For I could not be sure whether for the
rest of my life I would be able to tell when it was really my
mother and when it was really her shadow standing between
me and the rest of the world.

From Annie John *by Jamaica Kincaid*

I should be as happy here as the day is long, if I could hope
that I had your smile, your blessing, your sympathy upon
it. . . .

Florence Nightingale, English nurse

As I look at my daughters . . . I am astounded at what they accomplish. They are better mothers than I was and they are the admitted equals of their husbands in intelligence and initiative.

ANNE MORROW LINDBERGH, *American writer and aviator*

What *do* girls do who haven't any mothers to help them through their troubles?

From Little Women *by* LOUISA MAY ALCOTT

I have great, wild hopes of finding my daughter as she will be in adulthood, when she nominally stops needing me, when she is past the seizures and denunciations that I expect will come at adolescence because they came so brutally for me. . . . I hope that she needs me enough to show me who she is, to give regular dispatches, her intellectual progeny, and to trust me with their safekeeping.

NATALIE ANGIER, *American writer*

How are we to be the mothers we want our daughters to
have, if we are still sorting out who our own mothers are
and what they mean to us?

LETTY COTTIN POGREBIN, American writer

I have heard daughters say that they do not love their mothers.
I have *never* heard a mother say she does not love her daughter.

NANCY FRIDAY, American writer

Mothers of daughters are daughters of mothers and have
remained so, in circles joined to circles, since time began.

SIGNE HAMMER, author

To her whose heart is my heart's quiet home,
To my first Love, my Mother, on whose knee
I learnt love-lore that is not troublesome.

CHRISTINA ROSSETTI, English poet

Even feminist mothers for whom the subject of motherhood is a passion seldom write candidly about it except abstractly or from the point of view of the daughter. This leaves a great hole in our knowledge that few are willing to fill.

ALIX KATES SHULMAN, American writer

She was more like a magical older sister, my mother, in those impressionable days when the soft clay of my personality was being sculpted.

GAIL GODWIN, American novelist

As I read [my mother's] early letters to her sister and to her husband Clive, I was astonished by a vitality that I had not known was there; it was like uncovering a spring of silver water. An earlier identity glowed tantalizingly through these pages and through other people's memories and allusions, calling to life the mother I had always wanted, and with whom so many had fallen in love. Such a woman had invented the vibrant colors and shapes that surrounded me.

ANGELICA GARNETT, English writer, painter, and sculptor

I long to put the experience of fifty years at once into your
young lives, to give you at once the key of that treasure chamber
every gem of which has cost me tears and struggles and prayers,
but you must work for these inward treasures yourselves.

HARRIET BEECHER STOWE, American writer,
in a letter to her twin daughters

My relationship with my mother is not good, and as our
lives accumulate it often seems to worsen. We are locked
into a narrow channel of acquaintance, intense and binding.
For years at a time there is an exhaustion, a kind of
softening, between us. Then the rage comes up again, hot
and clear, erotic in its power to compel attention.

VIVIAN GORNICK, American journalist and scholar

Oh my son's my son till he gets him a wife,
But my daughter's my daughter all her life.

DINAH MULOCK CRAIK, English poet

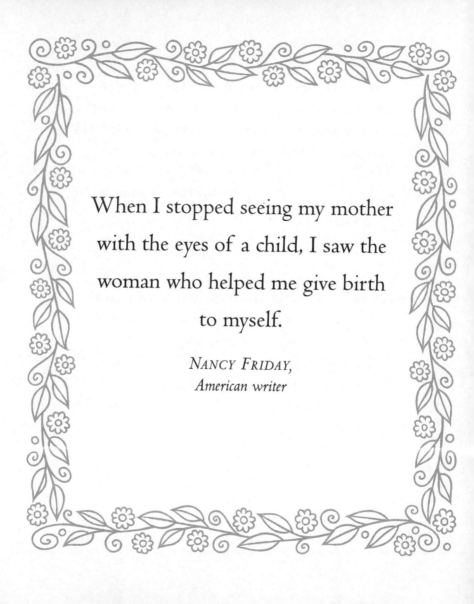

When I stopped seeing my mother with the eyes of a child, I saw the woman who helped me give birth to myself.

NANCY FRIDAY,
American writer

Our mothers and grandmothers have, more often than not, anonymously handed on the creative spark, the seed of the flower they themselves never hoped to see—or like a sealed letter they could not plainly read.

ALICE WALKER, American writer

Mummy herself has told us that she looked upon us more as her friends than her daughters. Now that is all very fine, but still, a friend can't take a mother's place. I need my mother as an example which I can follow. I want to be able to respect her.

ANNE FRANK, from her diary

The amicable loosening of the bond between daughter and mother is one of the most difficult tasks of education.

ALICE BALINT, psychoanalyst

What she is grows up out of her past in a becoming, natural way. She was born in a village where most women did not know how to read. She did not see a gaslight until she was twelve years old. And I? Am I perhaps what she herself might have become if she had been born in my generation in America?

KIM CHERNIN, American writer

Mothers and Sons

I must send you another birthday greeting and tell you how much I love you: that with each day I learn to extol your love and your worth more and that when I look back over my life, I can find nothing in your treatment of me that I would alter.

    LOUIS DEMBITZ BRANDEIS, *United States Supreme Court Justice*

Nobody can have the soul of me. My mother has had it, and nobody can have it again. Nobody can come into my very self again, and breathe me like an atmosphere.

    D. H. LAWRENCE, *English novelist and poet*

My mother was my first and toughest audience.

    ROBIN WILLIAMS, *American comedian and actor*

It takes a woman twenty years to make a man of her son,
and another woman twenty minutes to make a fool of him.

HELEN ROWLAND, American journalist and humorist

Fifty-four years of love and tenderness and crossness and
devotion and unswerving loyalty. Without her I could only
have achieved a quarter of what I have achieved, not only in
terms of success and career, but in terms of personal
happiness. . . . She has never stood between me and my life,
never tried to hold me too tightly, always let me go free. . . .

NOEL COWARD, British playwright

All that I am or hope to be, I owe to my angel mother.

ABRAHAM LINCOLN, 16th president of the United States

For a woman, a son offers the best chance to know the mysterious male existence.

CAROLE KLEIN, *American public relations executive*

I am persuaded that there is no affection of the human heart more exquisitely pure, than that which is felt by a grateful son towards a mother.

HANNAH MORE, *English writer and philanthropist*

I do not believe that I ever felt love for any mature person, except my mother, and even her I did not trust, in the sense that shyness made me conceal most of my real feelings from her.

GEORGE ORWELL, *English writer*

My mother made a brilliant impression upon my childhood life. She shone for me like the evening star. I loved her dearly.

WINSTON CHURCHILL, British statesman

With a mother of different mental caliber I would probably have turned out badly.

THOMAS ALVA EDISON, American inventor

There never was a woman like her. She was gentle as a dove and brave as a lioness.

ANDREW JACKSON, 7th president of the United States

Remember there is no one to whom I shall be prouder to tell of my successes or more willing to confess my failures.

ROBERT FALCON SCOTT, Antarctic explorer in a letter to his mother from the winter quarters of the British Antarctic Expedition

One of the great blessings of my life has been that I have had the good fortune to be able to share so much of it with my mother.

HENRY A. KISSINGER, German-born American statesman

If a man has been his mother's undisputed darling he retains throughout life the triumphant feeling, the confidence in success, which not seldom brings actual success with it.

SIGMUND FREUD, Austrian neurologist and father of psychoanalysis

Sons are the anchors of a mother's life.

SOPHOCLES, Greek playwright

If I have done anything in life worth attention, I feel sure
that I inherited the disposition from my mother.

> BOOKER T. WASHINGTON, *American educator*

It is odd how all men develop the notion, as they grow
older, that their mothers were wonderful cooks. I have yet to
meet a man who will admit that his mother was a kitchen
assassin, and nearly poisoned him.

> ROBERTSON DAVIES, *Canadian writer*

It seems to me that my mother was the most splendid
woman I ever knew. If I have amounted to anything, it will
be due to her.

> CHARLIE CHAPLIN, *English actor*

Happy he
With such a mother! Faith in womankind
Beats with his blood.

> ALFRED, LORD TENNYSON, *English poet*

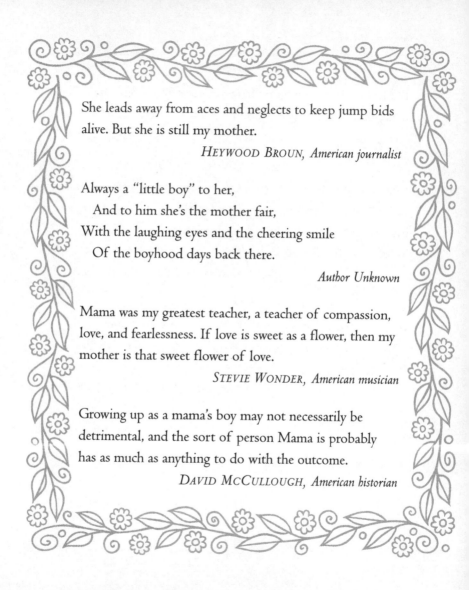

She leads away from aces and neglects to keep jump bids alive. But she is still my mother.

HEYWOOD BROUN, American journalist

Always a "little boy" to her,
  And to him she's the mother fair,
With the laughing eyes and the cheering smile
  Of the boyhood days back there.

Author Unknown

Mama was my greatest teacher, a teacher of compassion, love, and fearlessness. If love is sweet as a flower, then my mother is that sweet flower of love.

STEVIE WONDER, American musician

Growing up as a mama's boy may not necessarily be detrimental, and the sort of person Mama is probably has as much as anything to do with the outcome.

DAVID MCCULLOUGH, American historian

I remember how I clung to her till I was a great big fellow, but love of the best in womanhood came to me and entered my heart through those apron strings.

> *WOODROW WILSON, 28th president of the United States*

Mother's love shapes son's sense of belonging to the world.

> *WILLIAM WORDSWORTH, English poet*

Your letters always give me more strength, renewed courage and that bulldog tenacity so essential to the success of any man. There is no force that exerts the power over me that your letters do. I have learned to look forward to them so long and now when one is delayed, a spell of sadness and disappointment is cast over me.

> *LYNDON B. JOHNSON, 36th president of the United States*
> *in a letter to his mother written when he was a senior in college*

Boys are the best investment in the world. They pay the biggest dividends.

> *IDA EISENHOWER, mother of President Dwight D. Eisenhower*

When the going gets rough, my son and I can't call it quits
and cut our losses. I can't pack a bag, make a break for it,
find a more compatible child. The contract cannot be
broken.

SALLIE TISDALE, American writer and editor

That's the kind of mother to have, the kind I had,
credulous, superstitious, beautiful, comic, heroic, a rare
woman whom I seem never to have loved much or honored
enough.

ALFRED EDGAR COPPARD, English writer

You have been the best mother and I believe the best woman
in the world.

DR. SAMUEL JOHNSON, British lexicographer,
critic, and conversationalist

I hope that somehow I am and will be a wonderful mother for Sam . . . I want him to grow up to have a lot of faith and to be a very gentle person, and also to be militantly on his own side, as I have come to be. I hope he grows up to be caring and amused and political, someone who does not give up on the ideals of peace and justice and mercy for everyone.

ANNE LAMOTT, American writer

A son will be a leader of men, a soldier, a creator; he will bend the world to his will, and his mother will share his immortal fame; he will give her the houses she has not constructed, the lands she has not explored, the books she has not read.

SIMONE DE BEAUVOIR, French writer and philosopher

My mother said to me, "If you become a soldier you'll be a general; if you become a monk you'll end up as the pope." Instead, I became a painter and wound up as Picasso.

PABLO PICASSO, Spanish artist

How fortunate I am that my son, now a man, is today my dear and close friend.

RUTH BADER GINSBURG, *United States Supreme Court Justice*

Despite my mom's relentless chiding for eating too quickly and talking too much sports, I do not hesitate to use a phrase that up until now I have reserved for only those of my generation: She's one of my best friends.

WINSTON BAO LORD, *American television producer*

My mother, who is between seventy and eighty, is *much* younger than I am.

GEORGE BERNARD SHAW, *English playwright*

Mothers' expectations for their sons are thought to be different from all other earthly ones. As many men see it, life itself is a Sisyphean task of trying to meet their expectations.

LINDA R. FORCEY, *American educator*

My mother loved me completely and selflessly, and her
special legacy was a quiet, inner peace, and the
determination never to despair.

RICHARD MILHOUSE NIXON, 37th president of the United States

My son is wiser than I. He doesn't worry—just lives. His
vision is unclouded by prejudice. When innocence gives way
to a more complicated learning, I hope he'll grip fast to joy
and, clear-eyed, view the world with compassion.

JEWELL PARKER RHODES, American writer

Darling Mama, I had always prayed to show my love by
doing something famous for you. . . . Nothing you ever did
to me was anything but loving. I have no memories but love
and devotion.

GEORGE S. PATTON JR., American general

Mother deserves more credit than she gets. She is the one who was there. She is the one who read to us, who took us to Plymouth Rock and the Old North Church and other historic places. She gave me my interest in history.

JOHN F. KENNEDY, 35th president of the United States

I didn't bring him up to be president, but I'm not surprised. Of course, this is a mother talking, but from the first time I looked into his eyes, none of his accomplishments have surprised me.

REBEKAH BAINES JOHNSON, mother of Lyndon B. Johnson

One of the reasons he had never married was that he had held the memory of his mother very close. She had been soft with him far beyond what was usual in that place. Most of the women around had many children, but she had been widowed when she had only one child, and William was her pride and joy.

He learned tenderness from her.

From My Dream of You *by NUALA O'FAOLAIN*

Mothers-in-law

Belle-Mere. The French chose this word to give to the mother-in-law. It means beautiful mother. I wish all nations would adopt it. And it would be nice if comedians could get along without their tired tasteless jokes about mothers-in-law. It would be especially nice for mothers-in-law.

MARLENE DIETRICH, German-born American actor

Happy is she who marries the son of a dead mother.

Scottish Proverb

She was to me all that a mother could be, and I yield to none in admiration for her character, love of her virtues, and veneration for her memory.

ROBERT E. LEE, American general, about his mother-in-law

Quite nice women suddenly have to wear this title with the stigma on it and a crown of thorns. We're so frightened of it that we change our nature to avoid it and in so doing we end up the classical mother-in-law we feared in the first place; so gravely have we twisted ourselves.

SYLVIA ASHTON-WARNER, New Zealand educator

Never rely on the glory of the morning or the smile of your mother-in-law.

Japanese Proverb

She was a grand lady. When I hear these mother-in-law jokes I don't laugh. They are not funny to me because I've had a good one.

HARRY S. TRUMAN, 33rd president of the United States

I remember the first time I met her. She saw me as a potential enemy. Yes, it was actually fear I saw on her face. It was just that I was the first person he was serious about—Lyndon was also the strongest oar on the ship of her life. . . . I was trying to reassure this gentle—but very strong—woman that she had nothing to fear from me. She felt her son was too impetuous—and I kind of agreed.

LADY BIRD JOHNSON, American first lady

Miss Lillian was always, by sheer force of personality, the strongest link that held together her collection of strong-willed and independent children, in-laws, and grandchildren.

ROSALYNN CARTER, American first lady, about her mother-in-law

Behind every successful man stands a proud wife and a surprised mother-in-law.

BROOKS HAYS, American humorist

My dear Bird, I earnestly hope that you will love me as I do you. . . . It would make me very happy to have you for my very own, to have you turn to me with love and confidence, to let me mother you as I do my precious boy.

REBEKAH BAINES JOHNSON,
in a letter to her daughter-in-law, Lady Bird Johnson

I had to decide early on as a daughter-in-law that you can't beat her—you have to sit back and enjoy her. When I was a new bride, she beat me in paddle tennis with her right hand, then with her left. She is an extraordinary woman. She brings out the best in us.

BARBARA BUSH, American first lady

I might've been intimidated a little bit [because] this was—and is—the smartest woman I've ever encountered. Oh, Lord, yes, I confess that for me, Hillary has been a growth experience. I love her dearly now.

VIRGINIA CLINTON KELLEY,
about her daughter-in law Hillary Clinton

Family Portraits

I cannot forget my mother. Though not as sturdy as others, she is my bridge. When I needed to get across, she steadied herself long enough for me to run across safely.

RENITA WEEMS, American writer

My mother was a great reader, and with ten minutes to spare before the starch was ready would begin the *Decline and Fall*—and finish it, too, that winter. Foreign words in the text annoyed her and made her bemoan her want of a classical education—she had only attended a Dame's school during some easy months—but she never passed the foreign words by until their meaning was explained to her, and when next she and they met it was as acquaintances, which I think was clever of her.

J. M. BARRIE, English playwright

I had the most satisfactory of childhoods because Mother, small, delicate-boned, witty, and articulate, turned out to be exactly my age.

KAY BOYLE, American writer

My mother was the brains of the family—an avid reader and a passionate polemicist who had a love affair with ideas. She preceded us at the high school we attended where she earned a reputation as a very bright and gifted student. I was proud of my mother's mind.

GLORIA JEAN WADE-GAYLES, American poet and literary scholar

My Mother
She was as good as goodness is,
Her acts and all her words were kind,
And high above all memories
I hold the beauty of her mind.

FREDERIC HENTZ ADAMS, poet

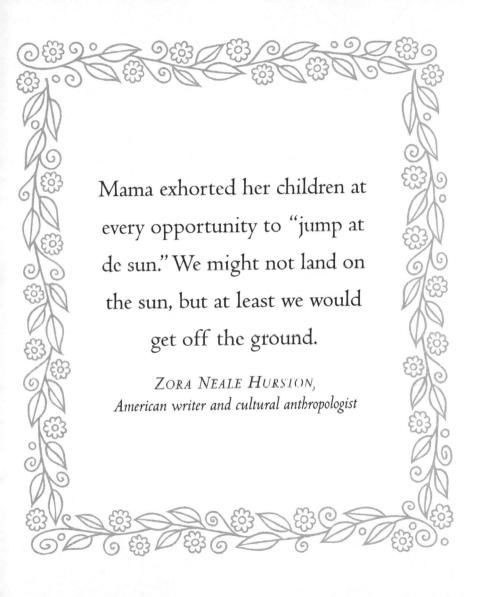

Mama exhorted her children at every opportunity to "jump at de sun." We might not land on the sun, but at least we would get off the ground.

ZORA NEALE HURSTON,
American writer and cultural anthropologist

My mother read her favorite poems out loud, would make us read plays together and acted herself. . . . Her reading out loud demanded the whole room, and while young her grace and dancing caught everyone's attention. Later it was her voice, her stories with that husky wheezing laugh that almost drowned out the punch lines.

MICHAEL ONDAATJE, *Sri Lankan-born Canadian novelist and poet*

My mother was the most perfect and magnetic character, the rarest combination of practical, moral, and spiritual, and the least selfish, of all and any I have ever known, and by me O so much the most deeply loved.

WALT WHITMAN, *American poet*

My mother was a wit, but never a sentimental one. Once, when somebody in our house stepped on our cat's paw, she turned to the cat and said sternly, "I *told* you not to go around barefoot."

ZERO MOSTEL, *American actor*

My mother read to me. She read to me in the big bedroom in the mornings, when we were in her rocker together, which ticked in rhythm as we rocked, as though we had a cricket accompanying the story. She'd read to me in the dining room on winter afternoons in front of the coal fire . . . and at night when I'd got in my own bed. I must have given her no peace. Sometimes she read to me in the kitchen while she sat churning, and the churning sobbed along with *any* story.

EUDORA WELTY, American novelist

In her own way though my mother was enlightened. Even at that time, she was a suffragist, as they called certain women's libbers in those days. Her answer to war was that all women should unite and resolve not to live with their husbands until they had made peace. Only women, she would say, could end war forever.

ISAAC BASHEVIS SINGER, Polish-born American writer

Mother had a thousand thoughts to get through with in a day, and . . . most of these were about avoiding disaster.

NATALIE KUSZ, American writer

She knew how to make virtues out of necessities.

AUDRE LORDE, West Indian-born American poet,
writer, and educator

Muv had invented a method of teaching which obviated the necessity for examinations. We simply read the passage to be mastered, then closed the book and related whatever portion of the text we happened to retain. "I always think a child only needs to remember the part that seems important to her," she would explain vaguely.

JESSICA MITFORD, English writer and journalist

My mother had a slender, small body, but a large heart—a heart so large that everybody's grief and everybody's joy found welcome in it, and hospitable accommodation.

MARK TWAIN, American writer

She was the light and not the lamp.

JESSAMYN WEST, American writer

One of the most charming things about Mother was the extraordinary patience with which she would allow us youngsters to "instruct" her. I remember my brother Hugh, when he was about eight, sitting on the foot of Mother's bed and giving her a half-hour lecture which began with the portentous question, "Mom, how much do you know about the common housefly?"

JEAN KERR, American playwright and writer

She did not understand how her father could have reached such age and such eminence without learning that all mothers are as infallible as any pope and more righteous than any saint.

> *From* The Hard-Boiled Virgin *by* FRANCES NEWMAN

The habit of worry had settled so firmly into her mother's being that her worries were her aspects of love.

> BESSIE BREUER, *American writer*

Her face beamed and rippled with mirth as before, and her laugh, that I had tried so hard to force, came running home again. I have heard no such laugh as hers save from merry children; the laughter of most of us ages, and wears out with the body, but hers remained gleeful to the last, as if it were born afresh every morning.

> J. M. BARRIE, *English playwright*

When my first novel came out, my mother injudiciously showed me some letters she had received from friends, making it clear that she had written to them apologizing for the sex scenes I had written, curse words I had used. "Well, you know," I overheard her once say on the phone, "you have to put that in, or your books don't sell."

JANET BURROWAY, novelist, poet, and playwright

Mama seemed to do only what my father wanted, and yet we lived the way my mother wanted us to live.

LILLIAN HELLMAN, American playwright and writer

Oh she made magic, she was a magic woman, my Mama. She was not wise in the world but she had magic wisdom.

LUCILLE CLIFTON, American poet

She was probably the stronger of my two parents. She taught us to go out and learn the white man's ways, and experience living in the non-Indian world. But she said we should never forget where we came from and where we have been.

PETERSON ZAH, president of the Navajo Nation

From my mother I learned the value of prayer, how to have dreams and believe I could make them come true.

RONALD REAGAN, 40th president of the United States

When a cake was in the oven an aura of mystery fell over the house. The shades were drawn, windows shut, neighbors informed. Mama moved cautiously about in house slippers. She knew nothing about thermodynamics. She knew only that a sponge cake is supposed to rise slowly and that the slightest sneeze within an area of twenty miles could cause a collapse.

SAM LEVENSON, American writer and humorist

My mother was at her best caring for the sick. She radiated calm.

JILL KER CONWAY, Australian-born American educator and writer

My mother was not just an interesting person, she was interested.

JOYCE MAYNARD, American writer

When someone asks you where you come from, the answer is your mother. . . . When your mother's gone, you've lost your past. It's so much more than love. Even when there's no love, it's so much more than anything else in your life. I did love my mother, but I didn't know how much until she was gone.

From One True Thing *by ANNA QUINDLEN*

She was ambitious not only for our success but for our souls. From our youth, we remember how, with effortless ease, she could bandage a cut, dry a tear, recite from memory "The Midnight Ride of Paul Revere," and spot a hole in a sock from a hundred yards away.

EDWARD KENNEDY, American senator

My mother was an authority on pig sties. "This is the worst-looking pig sty I have ever seen in my life, and I want it cleaned up now."

BILL COSBY, American comedian and actor

[My mother] said that I must always be intolerant of ignorance but understanding of illiteracy. That some people, unable to go to school, were more educated and more intelligent than college professors.

MAYA ANGELOU, American writer and poet

My mother wasn't what the world would call a good woman. She never said she was. And many people, including the police, said she was a bad woman. But she never agreed with them, and she had a way of lifting up her head when she talked back to them that made me know she was right.

BOX-CAR BERTHA, American hobo

Mother had a lot to say. This does not mean she was always talking but that we children felt the wells she drew upon were deep, deep, deep. Her theme was happiness: what it was, what it was not; where we might find it, where not; and how, if found, it must be guarded. Never must we confound it with pleasure. Nor think sorrow its exact opposite.

From "Happiness" by MARY LAVIN

At the age of eighty my mother had her last bad fall, and after that her mind wandered free through time. Some days she went to weddings and funerals that had taken place half a century earlier. On others she presided over family dinners cooked on Sunday afternoons for children who were now gray with age. Through all this she lay in bed but moved across time, traveling among the dead decades with a speed and ease beyond the gift of physical science.

RUSSELL BAKER, American journalist

The longer one lives in this hard world motherless, the more a mother's loss makes itself felt.

JANE WELSH CARLYLE, Scottish poet and letterwriter

The woman who bore me is no longer alive, but I seem to be her daughter in increasingly profound ways.

JOHNETTA B. COLE, American anthropologist

My mother had died when I was seven. For many years I lived primarily to search for her.

JANE LAZARRE, American writer

My mother was dead for five years before I knew that I had loved her very much.

LILLIAN HELLMAN, American playwright and writer

I acknowledge the cold truth of her death for perhaps the first time. She is truly gone, forever out of reach, and I have become my own judge.

SHEILA BALLANTYNE, American writer

Time is the only comforter for the loss of a mother.

JANE WELSH CARLYLE, Scottish poet and letterwriter

My mother always found me out. Always. She's been dead for thirty-five years, but I have this feeling that even now she's watching.

NATALIE BABBITT, American writer

Her beauty—for I know now it was beauty—was too elusive and fine for a child to appreciate: I only thought she was lovely because I loved her.

ELIZABETH BOWEN, Irish-American novelist

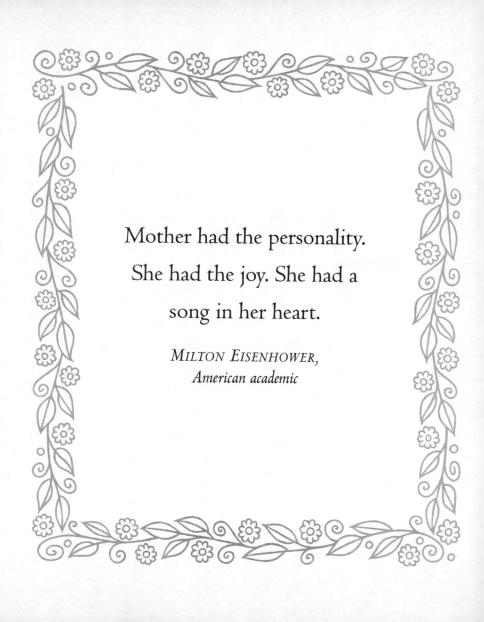

Mother had the personality.
She had the joy. She had a
song in her heart.

MILTON EISENHOWER,
American academic